It's So Easy!

Michael SB Reid

MICHAEL REID
—MINISTRIES—

Alive UK
Michael Reid Ministries
49 Coxtie Green Road
Brentwood
Essex CM14 5PS
England

ISBN 978-1-871367-31-7

All scripture quotations are taken from the
King James Version of the Bible.

ACKNOWLEDGEMENTS

To the late Demos Shakarian, a true and faithful minister, who was so instrumental in leading me to Christ

To the late Archbishop Benson Idahosa for his continued encouragement when we fellowshipped together.

To TL Osborn, an inspiration and a true example to me.

To all those who have had helped compile this book, I am forever grateful.

To God be the glory!

DEDICATION

To the body of believers worldwide and to those whom God will add – those who realise that Salvation is the Gift of God!

"For by grace are ye saved through faith; and that not of yourselves: it is the gift of God." (Ephesians 2:8)

Contents

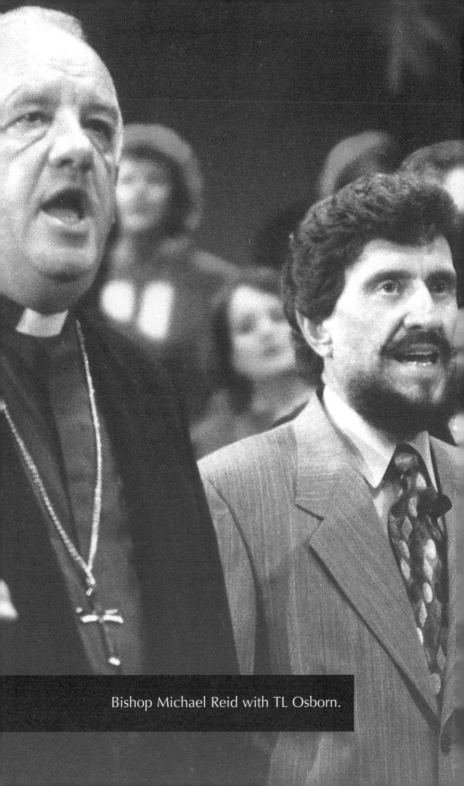
Bishop Michael Reid with TL Osborn.

Foreword

A high-caste Brahman Hindu gentleman said to a Christian: *"I don't like the Christ of your creeds and of your churches. But I am interested in Christ seated by the wayside, healing the blind, putting His hands on unclean lepers, and healing them — the one you Christians tell us arose from the dead, who came back to life so He could keep helping people. I could love and follow that Christ today. When I look at the Jesus you talk about, I think I can see how God is, and if that is how He is, He has my heart forever."*

I've lived my life sharing the gospel of Jesus Christ with multitudes of people in over ninety nations, always out on open terrain, in stadiums, ball parks, in auditoriums and out in public parks where all people of all faiths, or of no faith, can come and hear about Jesus Christ and learn of His love.

The Bible says, *"The gospel is the power of God unto salvation to everyone that believeth."*

Millions of Hindus, Muslims, Shintoists, Animists, and people who do not believe in God at all, have amassed themselves on these great fields, curious to hear what this foreigner might have to say about his god or gods.

I live with two visions before me: 1) The immeasurable gifts of Love and of Life that have been freely provided for humanity through the death, burial, resurrection and ascension of Jesus Christ; and 2) The multiplied millions of empty, bewildered, searching and confused people who populate this planet who have never heard about those immeasurable gifts of God's grace.

The author of this book was one of those empty and

hopeless persons, operating as a policeman, but concealing a spiritual bewilderment, adrift in a perplexed and empty confusion about God or the gods.

But a common businessman from California, while visiting London, was guided to this bewildered man by the Spirit of the Lord who said: *"Go get that man; I have a work for him to do!"*

This story of his conversion and subsequent global miracle ministry is *unique*. Read it and discover, afresh, the wonder of God's grace and love.

TL Osborn

An esteemed evangelist, statesman, teacher, author and publisher, known worldwide for his mass miracle ministry to millions, Dr TL Osborn has proclaimed the Gospel to more than 80 nations. Having evangelised in non-Christian nations for more than half a century, it is no wonder that Dr TL and his late wife, Dr Daisy Osborn, are said to have preached to more people, and witnessed more healing miracles, than any other couple in history!

Bishop Michael Reid & Ruth Reid.

Preface

Dear Reader

Our God is a good God. He loves you, He cares for you and He is waiting for you to stop struggling and striving and to believe in His provision. *"For by grace are ye saved through faith; and that not of yourselves: it is the gift of God" (Eph 2:8).*

When you believe in the free gift, His Son, Jesus Christ, that has already been sent for you, you can open your heart and believe what He has done for you. This happened two thousand years ago. God loves you. He showed it when He sent His only begotten Son to earth. Believe in His love and receive the gift of abundant life. He has done everything necessary to save and heal you right now.

Paul asked the question of the Galatian church, *"Who hath bewitched you, that ye should not obey the truth? ..." (Gal. 3:1).* Many people enter into life by the simplicity of the word of faith preached in the power of the Spirit but then lose sight of the fact that we need to live by the simplicity of what God has said.

Jesus said, *"If ye continue in my word then are ye my disciples indeed; and ye shall know the truth, and the truth shall make you free" (Jn. 8:31-32).*

Continuing in the word, rather than falling into legalism and a religious life of works in order to justify ourselves is leaving the very essence of our faith. The just shall live by faith. We're saved by the grace of God, nothing to do with us, it's a gift.

We've become partakers of the divine nature and we need

to say with Paul, *"I am crucified with Christ: nevertheless I live; yet not I, but Christ liveth in me: and the life which I now live in the flesh I live by the faith of the Son of God, who loved me, and gave himself for me" (Gal. 2:20).*

We're dependent on Him. It is so important to live in the simplicity of what Christ has done for us. He is our Redeemer, our Saviour, our Lord and our King.

As you read this book, let the words of truth penetrate your heart.

Should you need any help, please visit our website (www.MichaelReidMinistries.org) or contact the church prayer line (UK: +44 1277 372996 or USA: 918-491-2078). We are here as an expression of God's love to you. You can have a new start in life and know that you don't have a past, you have a glorious future.

Your friend,
Michael Reid

It's So Easy!

Police Constable Michael Reid.

1

It's Real!

There is nothing worse for a man who is 'fighting' God than to have well-meaning Christians attempt to share their religion with him. Worse still, is his realisation of the bankruptcy of religion and the sheer hypocrisy of it. What he is crying out for is a reality that really works and meets his innermost needs. He doesn't need another philosophy or teaching on 'self-actualisation.' He needs to be able to see the reality of a living witness moving in the power of life that only Spirit-filled believers have. I know, I was that man!

It was in 1965 that the world into which I was born changed dramatically for me. I want to share just what happened when a sceptic was confronted by undeniable miracles and an abundant life of joy and reality.

I had been in the police for some two and a half years and lived in a Section House (local police accommodation for unmarried police officers) in the heart of London. My life consisted of working in special crime squads at West End Central, Saville Row, London. Often I was in court by ten in the morning, having worked until three that morning. My job was my life and I was devoted to it. Yet hidden deep within was a desire for something different; inside was a discontent with the state of society.

The turning point came one night when I was called to a pub where a man had just been shot. He was in his twenties, just a barman who was suddenly confronted by a gunman who told him to open the cash register. He hesitated and was shot at point blank range. The gunman fled and I arrived to find the barman dying on the floor and a crowded pub full of late night revellers so shocked, they didn't know what to do. They had just witnessed a callous murder before their eyes and didn't know how to respond.

After the witnesses had been transported to the Police Station, I was left in the pub searching for the bullet that had passed through the barman's body and was supposedly lodged in the wall opposite. Whilst waiting for the coroner to pick up the body, I sat on a stool sipping a large scotch and watching the crime scene photographer taking pictures.

The landlady was pacing up and down the bar muttering, "How am I going to get this stain out of the carpet so I can open tomorrow? The blood's everywhere!"

I just sat there thinking, "What on earth is life all about? One moment you're alive and happy and suddenly your life is cut off in a second. What is the meaning of life?"

I replenished my glass and tried to forget the thousand questions that bombarded my mind.

It was a few days later that a couple of colleagues came up to me and suggested that I should go along to a meeting in The New Gallery, Regent Street, where some Americans were to speak. They told me that God spoke in those meetings.

My response was, "You're crazy! There is no God and I'll

prove it to you. They must be conmen. I'll come and show you where the microphones and loudspeakers are hidden. You wait and see ... There is no God!"

So, with determination, I agreed to go to the meeting to prove them wrong.

It was seven o'clock on a Tuesday night when I wandered into The New Gallery. There weren't many people there yet, so I had a good chance to check out the building and look for what I expected to find – hidden microphones and loudspeakers. All of a sudden, one of the organisers of the meeting came up to me and asked if I was a policeman and if my nickname was 'Tiger.'

My response was, "Yes it is; so what?"

"Well," he said "a lot of the young people from the area don't want to come in because you're here and they reckon you're going to 'nick' them. Will you give me your word that you won't 'nick' anyone, so I can reassure them that it's safe for them to come in?"

I laughed and said, "Sure. I won't 'nick' anyone. I'm just here to see what happens." But, inside myself, I thought, "What a sucker! I'll 'nick' who I want, when I want."

It seems strange looking back to think that I was expecting a booming voice around the auditorium, saying, "THIS ... IS ... GOD!" – and then whatever else he wanted to say! Now I see it was just crazy, but at the time I had no concept of how God spoke.

As I was standing in the hall waiting for the meeting to begin, another of the organisers came up to me and began to twitter on about God being real. He really got 'in my face.'

After a few seconds, I pushed him back against a wall and

said, "I worship the golden calf that Aaron made. Now, beat it, Buster!" (except my language was slightly more colourful).

He was shocked, and retreated to the far side of the hall.

The meeting began with people getting up and sharing how Jesus Christ had met them and changed their lives: some had been drug addicts, some alcoholics, some prostitutes, and others gang leaders. I watched and began to wonder what power it was that could get a heroin addict to change his life. I'd seen so many just get worse until they overdosed. I knew there was no answer for the kind of people we locked up and yet here were people saying this lifestyle was their past and now they had a new lifestyle in Christ. When the meeting closed, I spoke to one or two of the addicts to check out that they had really been mainliners. I was curious. How could a God who didn't exist do such things? Was there really an answer for life's needs?

Unexpectedly, a big Texan, wearing a ten-gallon hat, tapped me on the shoulder and asked me, "Are you a policeman called 'Tiger?' We are over here from the States to share the gospel. You're a police officer. Would you come and talk about the problems you face in dealing with people like this?"

I replied, "Sure."

He told me the meeting was in a couple of days' time at The Metropolitan Tabernacle which was in the Elephant and Castle area of inner London. He said that there were people he'd like me to meet to explain to them the problems of inner city London. He never mentioned Jesus and he didn't try and preach to me. He just gave me an invitation to the meeting.

Two nights later I went to The Metropolitan Tabernacle and sat some ten or fifteen rows back. I listened to testimonies from people who had been delivered by the power of Christ from drug addiction and all sorts of messed up lives. I found it fascinating because I knew society had no answers for people like that. Once they got on 'skid row' the only way was down!

During the meeting an Afro-American woman by the name of Mrs Simpson, got up to sing. I remember her singing,

> *"On a hill far away stood an old rugged cross*
> *The emblem of suffering and shame*
> *And I love that old cross, where the dearest and best*
> *For a world of lost sinners was slain"*

As she sung, tears began to flow down her cheeks and all of a sudden she began singing in a strange language (I had no idea what 'tongues' was, I thought she was singing in her native dialect). All I can say is, at that moment, I knew God was real (I now understand that 'tongues' is a sign for the unbeliever). I just knew God was real!

A collection was taken and as the plate came towards me down the row I heard a voice say, "Give all that you have and the Lord will provide."

I turned to see who it was that spoke with me and then realised it was a voice within. I took my wallet out of my pocket and emptied it into the collection plate. It just seemed the right thing to do. After that there was an altar call and people went forward.

I didn't move, but the Texan in the ten-gallon hat, whom I later found out to be Demos Shakarian, founder of the Full Gospel Businessmen's Fellowship International, came straight towards me and said, "Come on, I've got people I want you to meet." (It was some twelve years later that he told me God had spoken to him that night, pointed me out at the end of the meeting, and said to him, "Go get that man. I have a work for him to do." He left everyone on the platform to come and find me).

As we walked to the front of the hall, a woman was being prayed for and crashed to the floor.

I gingerly walked round her, as Demos laughed and said, "Strong stuff this religion."

I didn't understand what was happening. I just knew it was real!

I was introduced to quite a few people by Demos and we chatted to them. The hall began to empty and Demos turned to me and said, "Come on, let's go get a coffee."

As we walked towards the doors I pulled his arm and said, "I want to say something."

We sat half way back in the hall and I said to him, "You know, I've listened to testimonies from drug addicts, alcoholics and criminals, and God has changed their lives. The truth is, I'm more bound than they are. I'm a policeman and meant to be an example in society and yet I'm more bound than them."

Demos looked at me, smiled and said, "Come on, let's get my wife and two friends and we'll go for coffee."

We walked to the back of the hall and met up with Earl Pickett and his wife, and Rose, Demos' wife, and I took them in my car back towards the Hilton Hotel in Park Lane, where they were staying. As I drove I listened to them laughing and joking. They were so happy and so full of joy. The only jokes I knew weren't the types of jokes I would want them to hear. There was an atmosphere of cleanness and joy, and how I wanted it. I realised I desperately wanted to be like them.

As we approached Park Lane and parked outside the Hilton, Demos said, "Let's go to The Steak House just down the road and get some food."

We went in and sat down. I ordered a T-bone steak, as did Demos, and as we sat there I suddenly realised that I had put all my money in the collection and couldn't have bought a meal that night. I heard that same quiet voice within saying, "See, I told you I'd provide."

During the meal, Earl Pickett shared his testimony with me and I began to see that God could truly change anyone, even me, and I really wanted Him to.

After the supper, we went into the hotel and up to Demos' room. They shared the gospel in such a simple way.

They asked me, "Did you know that Jesus died for you on Calvary's Tree?"

I said, "I have always believed that;" but for the first time in my life I knew it was true. (I'd been brought up in a public school which had chapels every morning so I was familiar with Bible stories, but not living faith).

They then asked me if I believed that Jesus rose from the dead on the third day.

I said, "I've always believed that;" but for the first time in my life I knew it to be true on the inside.

They suggested we pray. As they prayed a great feeling of joy welled up inside me. I wanted to laugh and laugh but I suppressed the feeling of joy because I didn't want to offend them. In the end, I felt I was going to burst with joy and began to pray inside, "Oh God, shut them up! Stop them!"

When they stopped I was relieved but so full of joy. I arranged to meet them for breakfast the next morning and left to go home. I drove my car back to the garage where I parked it and began to walk the short distance to the Section House. I was floating on air and suddenly realised I was singing at the top of my voice. I stopped and looked round to make sure no-one had seen me. It was three o'clock in the morning. I was alive! I couldn't go to bed. I ran a hot bath and sat in it with a little New Testament they'd given me. I remember I had to keep topping up the bath with hot water as I read.

The next morning I raced over to the Hilton to meet them for breakfast. I told them how wonderful it was and that I hadn't been able to sleep. I was so alive inside. It was like a ton weight had been lifted off me. I felt so free and so full of joy. During breakfast they told me that now I'd been saved I needed to be filled with the Holy Spirit. A man called Darrell Hon suggested we go and pray. We went up to his room and I asked how you received it.

He said, "It's not *it*, it's *Him*, the third person of the Godhead. Just ask Jesus and He will fill you with the Holy Spirit."

I knelt on the floor and shouted at the top of my voice, "JESUS, FILL ME!"

The feeling of joy I had the night before burst forth and I began to laugh and laugh. Suddenly, I found myself speaking in a language I had never learned. I tried it fast and slow, loud and soft, and I got up and tried it from every side of the room. I remember looking out of the window to see if the traffic was still going by. I was so full of joy that I didn't know what was happening to me. I just received the gift. I was a new man in Christ.

Over the next week, I spent my time with another member of Demos' team, Nicky Cruz, a New York gang leader who had been led to the Lord by Dave Wilkerson (author of "The

Cross and The Switchblade"). We spent two days and nights just talking and I realised there wasn't much difference between us; that God had plucked us both from the lowest point to His precious heights. It was so good to be able to share with people who understood the depths of despair and the realities of new life. I remember driving Demos and Rose to the airport and, as we said our goodbyes and they passed through security, I burst into tears. I couldn't help myself since the people who had become dearest to me were leaving and I felt I was left alone.

Demos said, "Don't worry. God will take care of you," but I wasn't convinced.

I realised I could no longer stay in the police force. I wanted to do something for God with my life and so I went to see my superintendent at Saville Row in order to hand in my resignation. When I walked into his office I decided to give my testimony. I think, judging by his reaction, that he thought I'd gone out of my mind and said that I never need go on the streets again. I think it was probably to protect the public from me more than to help me! Many in the Section House couldn't believe that I'd really been converted and thought there was some ulterior motive; though I shared, they didn't understand. It seemed so impossible that someone like me could change overnight, but I had!

Over the years I can look back and realise the truth that *"by grace are ye saved through faith; and that not of yourselves: it is the gift of God (Eph. 2:8)."* God found me. He met me. He changed me. He healed me. He transformed me. It was all of Him and I can lay claim to none of it. Grace – undeserved favour – is the very foundation of all salvation. Where sin abounds, grace does much more abound, and thank God it abounded for me!

I left behind the old life to begin a new. Everything within me was different. Salvation had come to my house: the old had gone, the new had come. A new chapter of my life had begun.

> *On a hill far away stood an old rugged cross,*
> *The emblem of suffering and shame;*
> *And I love that old cross where the dearest and best*
> *For a world of lost sinners was slain.*
>
>> *So I'll cherish the old rugged cross,*
>> *Till my trophies at last I lay down;*
>> *I will cling to the old rugged cross,*
>> *And exchange it some day for a crown.*
>
> *O that old rugged cross, so despised by the world,*
> *Has a wondrous attraction for me;*
> *For the dear Lamb of God left His glory above*
> *To bear it to dark Calvary.*
>
> *In that old rugged cross, stained with blood so divine,*
> *A wondrous beauty I see,*
> *For 'twas on that old cross Jesus suffered and died,*
> *To pardon and sanctify me.*
>
> *To the old rugged cross I will ever be true;*
> *Its shame and reproach gladly bear;*
> *Then He'll call me some day to my home far away,*
> *Where His glory forever I'll share.*

(George Bennard , 1913)

"The man of faith is totally outside of legalism."

2

Bond or Free?

ooking back, from the moment of my new birth, God gave me a real hunger for knowledge of Himself. As a result, I avidly read and studied the Bible, as well as many books written by men and women who were inspired of God through the centuries. It was my fellowship with the Bible and the books of old which was the most significant influence on my development as a Christian.

After Demos left, I started to search for others who had the same living reality that he and I had both received. I visited churches in my immediate area; I could find no-one who really had that same life. I went to a church where everyone could tell me exactly what you had to do to be a Christian: read your Bible for so long each day, read this or that book, pray for so long, confess your sins so much, but everything seemed so ritualistic. What I'd seen when I first came into life was so, so different.

My search led me to the north of England, to a man whom I was told had all the answers. I went there thinking he really understood the ways of God but soon discovered, that although he had an idea of what was true, his theories were not reality. I watched many of those who tried to fulfill what he was teaching end up in a mess.

I remember saying to him one day, "Well, do you have what you're preaching?"

He said, "No. You preach the highest and hope people will come into it."

This man taught that there was some additional higher experience that would totally liberate a person from sin. Therefore many were seeking this experience.   He was instructing people in a legalistic form and telling them it would produce Christian perfection, and yet it was not reality. The more I realised this, the more I realised he was deceived; he preached one thing and lived another lifestyle.

Whilst in the north of England, I became involved in ministry.   Unfortunately political infighting for leadership developed amongst the elders of the church. They were also unhappy that when I prayed for people, miracles happened so easily. They called me critical but it was actually nothing to do with criticism; I just wanted to preach the simple gospel. Envy and jealousy are very destructive in any church. I felt very much that what they had to give was rather like the children's story of The Emperor with No Clothes. Everyone was pretending they'd got what they hadn't got.   Let me remind you of the story.

Once upon a time there lived a vain Emperor whose only worry in life was to dress in elegant clothes. He changed clothes almost every hour and loved to show them off to his people. One day, two rogues went to the Emperor, pretending to be weavers. They said they could make him a suit of fabric so fine that fools wouldn't be able to see it.   The Emperor agreed to let them make the suit. When it was finished the

Emperor tried on his new suit. The problem was, he couldn't see it.

However, he didn't want his subjects to know this because he would have to admit that he was a fool, so he thought, "I'll pretend that I can see it."

The servants couldn't see it either, even the Emperor's wisest adviser couldn't see it, but no one wanted to appear a fool so they didn't say anything.

The Emperor decided to wear it in a parade so all his subjects could see what a fine suit it was. Of course, he was wearing nothing at all as he walked down the street.

Nobody wanted to appear foolish so they didn't dare say anything, apart from a small boy who shouted, "Look! The Emperor is naked!"

Then everybody realised it was true but the Emperor, not wanting to admit his foolishness, continued with the parade as if nothing was wrong.

Many religious people are like this. They wear coats of religion which they pretend are beautiful but in reality they're wearing nothing. However, they're too ashamed to admit it! If what you have isn't real in your daily living, you are deceived and need to examine yourselves.

I went on holiday for a week and stayed in a caravan in North Wales. When I was in that caravan, God began to speak to me about the difference between the two seeds in the church: the seed of the bond and the seed of the free. I saw that the seed of the free (the man of faith) is totally outside of legalism. That man doesn't live believing that he can make himself righteous. He knows that he has the righteousness of Christ, imputed and imparted to him by faith and that what Christ did for him 2,000 years ago has purchased an inward reality that can't be put down. I saw that the religious man was diametrically opposed to the man of faith. The seed of the bond judged you on the externals: the way you behaved, the way you talked, the way you looked, the way you did things, but would totally ignore what was really the mark of a man of God, faith. The people of faith would always be rejected by the people of religion.

What I saw in some churches was a culture of legalism. It became my purpose in life to explain the difference between the seed of the bond and the seed of the free and look for those who understood the life of faith instead of the life of legalism. I discovered that some had begun in real faith but then ended up in law. God showed me that the freedom He gives doesn't bring license but it does set a totally different standard. It became obvious that the standard by which many Christians judged one another was nothing to do with Christianity, it was to do with their ethical codes and very often those codes were governed by their culture and humanistic values.

I found a hidden Christian culture as there was with the Pharisees and the Sadducees in Jesus' time. "This is the way we are. This is the way we dress. This is the way we eat. This is the way we talk. This is the way we define. This is the way we behave." It was legalism in the extreme and yet when I pointed it out to them they got offended because they were 'the people of faith.' They were not people of faith at all. They persecuted anyone that came with freedom, usually motivated by envy and jealousy because they lacked the power and authority themselves and hated to see someone else living in reality.

I remember being so joyful when the Holy Spirit met me. I went to a Christian Conference Centre where I met an old woman who'd been a missionary for 30 years in India.

She turned round after I'd been there three days and said, "Young man, it's not natural to be happy all the time."

She wasn't. She was bitter; both against God for her failure on the mission field and because she never got married. She could not bear the idea of someone else finding joy, happiness and reality. Her whole life was consumed by religion and talk of religious things. When I tried to tell her that the life of Christ is a life lived, not a set of rules kept and adhered to, she complained about me to the leaders.

To religious people, very often a person's outward actions seem so wrong and yet they're so right. I began to see that what was needed was the realisation that when Christ died for us, when He came and redeemed us, when He shed His precious blood for us, He actually took away the burden of the law from us, because He fulfilled the law. I found time and again that the law had been re-imposed, not as blatant legalism in terms of right and wrong in a harsh manner, but in a much more subtle way, almost a code of conduct. If you didn't meet the person's religious code, you'd had it. If you didn't use the right words, you'd had it. It was nothing to do with Christianity. Jesus pointed out that the Pharisees and Sadducees had turned the law of God into the precepts of man.

I found very few churches which brought people to a living Christ. They didn't seem to realise that a person could still be an individual. They tried to mould people to conform to their legalistic and ethical codes, without realising that it was legalism. They didn't understand the truth that when Christ comes the greatest gift that comes within a person is freedom; freedom to be free in Christ but also to be your own person.

Their understanding of life in Christ was being 'discipled' which meant conformity in the extreme, and by conformity they wanted uniformity.

They seemed to forget that God made us wonderfully individual. They failed to see that Peter, a fisherman, was always an impetuous man. Or that Paul, a scholar, was a man of diligence who was violent in his zeal in persecuting the church. God saved Paul but that same vehement desire was in him when he was filled with the Holy Spirit. God did not make him into a totally different person. The difference was the life of Christ within.

The Bible tells us that Abraham often referred to as our Father in the Faith, didn't conform. He left Mesopotamia; came out of his country and his family, and walked with his God. When he went among heathens they didn't really understand him. When Jesus came to His own people, they didn't receive Him. The reason they couldn't receive him was that He didn't conform to their expectations of what the Messiah should be like or the cultural norms of His day: "now you must wash your hands," "now you've got to do this," "If you knew who that woman was, you wouldn't talk to her." The whole way of religious thinking had a cultural bias to it, without any basis in love, in grace, or in truth. Anyone who's truly born again and filled with the Holy Spirit, experiences the same.

Take Smith Wigglesworth: the Assemblies of God today boast of him; however, in his lifetime they banned him from many churches because he didn't conform to their standards.

The same was true for the Maréchale, William Booth's eldest daughter (William Booth was the founder of the Salvation Army). She went to Paris and did a tremendous work of God and yet there was always friction because she didn't conform to the Salvation Army's structure. In the end the situation forced her to resign, and yet she was one of their most valuable officers.

It has happened time and again throughout history. George Whitefield was persecuted by the Methodists and in the end went to New England. The reason? He wouldn't conform to their ideas. People would listen to him preach for hours in the open air. He didn't preach legalism. He preached life, and there's such a difference.

When I tried to explain this to people I found that so few really wanted to hear. They were secure with their legalistic framework where they could determine whether God was happy with them or not. Their Christianity was not based on a relationship with the living God, but on adherence to a set of rules and regulations. They demanded conformity but I found it so deadly.

The Bible says that *"we have this treasure in earthen vessels, that the excellency of the power may be of God, and not of us" (2 Cor. 4:7)*. Christ had come to live inside, but the reality was, and this is where I differed so much from so many, that I was still me. God didn't want me to be someone else! He didn't want me to conform to a cultural norm. He didn't want me to conform to a basic standard that religious people called 'Christian.'

I discovered that the majority of people didn't care for the individual. What they cared for was the maintenance of their religion by their ethical code or culture through which they tried to make people conform to their style. They did not appreciate that freedom did not mean that we had lawlessness or iniquity; it meant that we had the life of Christ and that life was shown in a many-faceted way.

I thank God, when I came to Christ, I met Nicky Cruz who had been a gang leader. Nicky Cruz was not the average person you'd find in an evangelical church. Demos Shakarian was a dairy farmer and he remained a farmer. I remember one day, when he was sharing in a Full Gospel Businessmen's Fellowship International (FGBMFI) meeting he knocked over the milk he was drinking. He just put his foot on the chair and wiped his boot with the table cloth. He was a farmer, to him that was the natural thing to do, but some people were offended by him. They couldn't understand that a man could be like that. There was a kind of code where you couldn't be yourself. You had to be what they wanted you to be. Jesus wasn't like that. He was what He was.

I loved the FGBMFI meetings. Individuals would stand up and testify about how Christ had really impacted their lives. The meetings would be in a restaurant or hotel and people would come for a meal. The atmosphere wasn't at all religious so people felt comfortable having a good meal and fellowship with friends. The Holy Spirit moved in a tremendous way when those testifying expressed how God had met them. I saw many miracles of healing and beautiful conversions happen to people who would never have darkened the doors of a church, but felt secure in a businessmen's meeting. Demos Shakarian had a real vision for reaching the 'unchurched'; and they usually wouldn't go to a church to be reached! Christ sent us into the world to preach, teach and heal; not to indoctrinate and subordinate people.

The one thing I wanted was for people to be who they were in Christ; to let those natural gifts flow as the Holy Spirit filled them; to let God take them and use them in His own way, not in a way of conformity or uniformity, but in a way of freedom of life, with everyone taking their different positions because it was natural for them to take it.

3

Stacking the Chairs!

I've always found that when God speaks to the depths of your soul it is life transforming if you obey His voice. His interventions along life's walk are rare but wonderful. It has always bothered me when individuals seem to need continuous interventions by God. The Bible says if you turn to the left hand or the right you'll hear a voice behind you saying, *"this is the way, walk ye in it" (Isa. 30:21)*.

I left the ministry for a few years during which time I met my wife and moved to the South of England. I started a new job in London as a Marketing Director for a publishing company. I then moved and joined 'Save and Prosper' and became very successful as a salesman.

It was a day like any other day in 1976 that I went to my office in Ilford, Essex. About mid-morning I just felt to call on Rev. Trevor Dearing, a dear friend and evangelist, who lived nearby. He had a tremendous healing ministry and ran an organisation called "Power, Praise and Healing." He had been an Anglican minister who had built up a church in Hainault and was used of God to inspire the gift of healing. When I got to his house he was just taking something out of

Still a praising, rejoicing, and dancing church.

the boot of his car and we greeted each other.

He looked at me and said, "Michael, you have to start preaching again. If you don't start now you never will."

I knew at that moment it was God speaking to me and it was a challenge and an inspiration.

I had gone through years of seeing churches leap from one revelation to another. It was the time of the Discipleship Movement which caused great division amongst the churches in England. There was political skullduggery amongst the competing leaders and I well remember a day when these leaders met at the Royal Albert Hall claiming they were going to recognise and support each other. They claimed to be totally committed to each other. Sadly, this only lasted a few months.

In the midst of this atmosphere, as I contemplated God's direction to start preaching again, God spoke to me.

He clearly said, "You know what you don't want, now build what you do want!"

I knew at that point it was a call from The Most High to become a co-worker with Him in building His Church.

I knew that what I didn't want was the lack of reality that was evident in the majority of the churches in the country. I just didn't want that. I wanted something that was different. I wanted something where life was family and where family was life. I wanted a community of people who could love each other in truth and reality and know the living God in their midst; where they could see the miracles that Christ spoke of and not 'play games with gifts' but have the reality of the power of God within. I knew that it must be possible on earth to see the life of Christ in the midst of His people. I believe Jesus came to heal, to deliver and to bring life, but I also believe that He came for the lost. However, the thing that I wanted to avoid most of all was legalism.

My wife and I started a Bible Study in our home two mornings a week, starting at 7:00 am. At this point there were only three other people besides us. On Sundays we met in another home to praise God. Miracles of healing began to happen, attracting more and more people, and our numbers increased so that when we reached thirty it became clear we needed a hall to meet in.

On 14th November 1976 we officially became known as the Ongar Christian Fellowship and Trevor Dearing spoke at our first meeting. We began to look for suitable premises and soon found a room in The Arts and Activity Centre in the middle of Ongar, Essex. Within six months we had over 60 people meeting several times a week. Word rapidly spread of the miracles; many sick people came and God met them.

Because of my previous experience of church, we sung hymns from the Redemption Hymnal. Our pianist had a grand piano and we were really formal. Bible teaching was the most important part of the meeting. The miracles were beautiful but I felt something was lacking and I didn't know what it was.

One Tuesday night in September, in the middle of the meeting, God spoke to me and said, "Stop the meeting and stack the chairs up."

I was preaching at the time and can remember speaking back inside to God, saying, "Don't be ridiculous. We're in the middle of our meeting."

I carried on preaching and lovely miracles happened at the end of the meeting. On Friday, the same thing happened.

Once again I responded by saying, "We're having a

meeting."   Looking back, my comments seem absurd, but I didn't know what God had in store.

On the Sunday morning some sixty people gathered for our meeting in The Arts and Activity Centre. We began to sing the first hymn when once again the Lord came to me and said, "Stop the meeting and stack the chairs up."

We were in the middle of the first verse of the hymn so I told the pianist to stop playing.

I looked at the congregation and said, "I want you all to stack the chairs around the sides of the room."

They looked at me in surprise because we were just ready to begin the meeting. It took me some five minutes to persuade them to let go of the security of their chairs. I ended up with a group of people standing near the pile of chairs around the sides of the room looking at me and thinking I'd lost my mind. I encouraged them to come back towards the centre of the room and once again it took some coaxing.

"What on earth was the pastor going to do?" they must have been thinking.

I looked at them and could see the dubious looks on their faces as they stared at me. This had never happened before. They looked at me and I looked at them. I didn't know what to do next.

When you step out of the boat onto the troubled sea, you need to know that it is Jesus who called you to step out or you'll sink. I knew God had spoken but He had only told me to stack the chairs up; that was it.

As they looked at me, I said, "We're going to praise God."

I closed my eyes and lifted my hands to heaven. The only way I can describe what happened next is that 'all bedlam broke loose.' I opened my eyes to see some people falling to the ground, crying out for mercy; others leaping and dancing; others throwing their hymnbooks in the air; others shouting. I stood and watched God take the meeting for the next two and a half hours. I didn't interfere. He seemed to know what He was doing and I figured that if He had started it, He'd better finish it!

Many of the congregation told me afterwards they'd had visions of Heaven. They had seen angels dancing in their midst. They'd been healed and delivered and their lives transformed. The presence of God was so mighty that everyone was dramatically affected in one way or another. From that moment God had birthed His Church and I knew the gates of hell could not prevail against it.

For months afterwards, as soon as we began to sing, the glory of God would descend. If strangers came into the meeting, they either ran for the door or 'hit the deck' when the glory of God descended. It was exciting, since every meeting was different. Some mid-week nights, God would open the scriptures to us and I would have to persuade people to go home at midnight or one o'clock in the morning. The glory of God was so real they just wanted to stay. It was a visitation from God that birthed the family of God; for every true church is a family and every family is a small church.

Word soon spread that God had done something special with us and I was asked by a local minister to share with him what had happened. We went to lunch with him and his wife and I explained what had happened.

His question was simple, "What doctrine were you preaching? What Bible verse was it? We need to get all the local ministers to experience this."

I told him, "You can't. We stacked the chairs up; that's all. That's what God told us to do. You can't duplicate what God alone can do."

He got quite 'shirty' with me and our discussion got quite heated. He accused us of wanting to keep the move of God to ourselves. I pointed out that I only did what God told me to do and that I couldn't reproduce His moving.

At this point, his wife banged her knife and fork down on the table and said, "It's not fair. God promised to do it in our church, not yours!"

I looked at her, laughed, and said, "Well, maybe He got the wrong address!" It was sad to see envy and jealousy rear their heads. God is no respecter of persons. He does what He wants, when He wants, where He wants, how He wants.

Once God had visited us in this fashion, we became a dancing, praising and shouting church, full of joy, and the Word of God became mighty in our midst. Often, revelation would come and the preaching would go on for two or three hours. You could hear a pin drop and the presence of God was so tangible. People didn't want to move from their seats, they just sat and bathed in the wonderful presence of God, as the truth of God's Word overwhelmed them. The beauty of His grace and His wonderful love became the touchstone of a triumphant church. I suddenly realised that when God told me to build what I wanted, because I knew what I didn't want, I had learned the secret – to step aside and let Him build as I became a co-worker with Him. Jesus promised He would build His Church and that is the Church I want to belong to.

Today, some thirty years later, we have a property of 27 acres, which houses our church, our administration offices, the television department and a Bible College (affiliated with

Oral Roberts University, Tulsa, Oklahoma and in partnership with the University of Wales). Nearby we have 74 acres of beautiful parkland with a beautiful 18th century country mansion which houses our day school. The school is now academically one of the top schools in the country. God enabled us to buy our school and He's been so faithful in providing all we need.

We have many different nationalities in the church, people from every strata of life, and yet we are one body in Christ. Our culture is the culture of Heaven: one Lord, one faith, and one baptism. Who would have dreamed that stacking the chairs could have such dramatic results! Certainly not me!

My desire wasn't to try to bring people into a religion but to bring them into Christ. The church began with the simple occurrence of miracles because that's the way Jesus advertised His Church. "No miracles, … No Jesus!" When He was on earth the multitudes came because they saw the miracles that He did. They came because they had needs in their lives and they knew that He was going to meet those needs.

Bishop Michael Reid & Archbishop Benson Idahosa.

4

Find a 'Paul!'

I t's interesting to note how God brings people together in miraculous ways and causes their paths to cross. Elijah wasn't looking for Elisha; he just happened to be passing that way and there was Elisha ploughing with his father's yoke of oxen. Elisha wasn't looking for Elijah but God joined them when He told Elijah to throw his mantle on him.

Everyone needs such a father in the faith; someone that they can trust, that has proved themselves in the work that God has given them to do.

Early on in my ministry God spoke to me audibly, "Timothy, find a Paul to sit under, and learn from him."

I knew exactly what and who God meant so I packed all my belongings into my car and moved to the north of England where this man was. I spent the next two years learning as much as I could from him.

Through the years I've found that I haven't had to search for the right 'Paul.' God has brought the right men of God into my life at various times and all of them have been miraculous connections. Men such as Alf Schulters, Judson Cornwall, Benson Idahosa, T. L. Osborn and Oral Roberts have all have left an indelible mark on me. I could write a book about each of them, telling what our relationship has meant, both personally and in my ministry. Let me tell you about one of my dearest friends.

In 1986 I went to a conference in Minehead to hear a man called Archbishop Benson Idahosa from Benin City, Nigeria. I was attracted to attend when I heard God had raised the dead through him and had a tremendous miracle ministry. It seemed to me I could learn from this man. I sat in the meetings and was fascinated by the depth of faith he had, though I was appalled by the lack of response from so many who attended his meetings. He was so alive and real that I wanted to know more.

One meeting, as he was leaving the hall, I saw him crowded around by people filing out; they seemed to be ignoring him.

I pushed my way through and when I got to him I said, "Excuse me, you don't know me but I'd like you to come to my church."

He turned and looked at me and said, "You don't belong here!"

I responded, "Neither do you!"

He laughed and invited me back to his chalet to meet his wife. In that second we became firm friends. We talked for hours about the God we loved. I found he understood what God had done for us and he promised to come to my church the next week.

Three days after returning from the conference, I received a phone call. It was Benson, who was now in Liverpool.

He said to me, "I've cancelled the last three days of the meetings here. I'm coming to your church." And so he did.

The first meeting he came to, he walked into our building and found what he'd never expected to find in England. The praise, the rejoicing, and the dancing went on for an hour and a half. He kicked off his shoes and joined us in our adoration of a magnificent Saviour. He shared wonderful messages and truly became part of my life. From that time on, he visited us three or four times a year and for the next 10 years we travelled together to 15 nations around the world, ministering the gospel.

On about his third visit to the church, we walked into the building together. The people were already rejoicing and singing and praising God. Suddenly he became transfixed, almost like a statue. I couldn't get him to move. He was in mid-pace; just frozen to the spot. I carried on to the platform and led the meeting but I couldn't help looking at him every few seconds wondering what on earth had happened. After about seven to ten minutes, he just walked normally up to the platform and joined the meeting. When he preached he shared that God had transfixed him to the spot as he was walking in and spoken to him. The Holy Spirit had shown him that healing would flow in this church and people would come from all over the world to find that healing flow. He said we would be surprised at what God would do. He shared many things and truly every word that he prophesied has come to pass.

I remember Benson later telling me that God had told him to take myself as his son. He argued with God saying, "I've heard of a white man taking a black man as a son, but not a black man taking a white man!"

God's reply was, "I didn't know you were black and I didn't know Michael was white!"

That clinched it for Benson.

He was such a good friend to my wife and I. If we weren't travelling together, hardly a week passed when we didn't speak on the phone. We understood each other and became 'closer than brothers.' He was a man of faith who lived his life to the full, preaching in over 149 different nations, building over 6,000 churches with over 7 million members worldwide. He was a leader of leaders who loved his God and was a great encourager to those he met. He had time for everyone, from the least to the greatest, and had a compassion that few men have.

Often he would say to me, "You know, people will work you to death and when you're dead they'll never even put a rose on your coffin."

In March 1998 he was 'promoted to glory.' I went to his funeral in Benin City, Nigeria. For me, I'd lost a brother and my best friend. I managed to control my emotions until they came to inter (place) his coffin which bore the sole inscription, 'MAN OF FAITH.' They called the bishops forward, of whom I was one, and gave us each a rose to put on his coffin. When they did that, I could hold back my tears no longer; I could hear his voice saying, "They won't even put a rose on your coffin."

I laid my rose on his coffin and said, "This is for those who never came."

He was a man of whom the world was not worthy, a man of faith. He has left an indelible mark on the face of Nigeria, having transformed that nation through the authority that God gave him. But more than that, he left an indelible mark upon my life and the lives of all who knew him. What a man of joy and love he was - a true father in the faith!

If only we could trust God, like little children.

5

You Can't Earn It!

S o often in today's culture, the emphasis is on self-fulfilment, self-realisation, self-love and self-acceptance. Psychologists have done much damage by telling people to accept what they are no matter how perverse their lifestyle. Society has bred a culture of tolerance to all extremes, with one exception, an intolerance of anyone who has morals and ethics of biblical standards.

Hidden behind this vast façade is a very dangerous snare of the enemy. The Bible says that if we ask anything according to His will, He'll do it. Jesus taught His disciples to pray, *"Thy will be done on earth as it is in heaven" (Matt. 6:10).*

Prayer is communion with the living God which brings us into conformity to His will and desires. The scripture says that God causes us to will and to do of His good pleasure.

It is said of Jesus in Hebrews, *"Lo, I come (in the volume of the book it is written of me,) to do thy will, O God" (Heb. 10:7).*

He also said, *"The Son can do nothing of himself, but what he seeth the Father do. ..." (Jn. 5:19).*

To Jesus, true discipleship was denying yourself, taking up your cross and following Him. We are born again, not of the will of man, nor of the will of the flesh, but of God. How then can precious communion with the Father be turned into sessions where men seek to manipulate God to gain their own will and desires?

Many years ago, I was speaking at a conference for pastors in Atlanta. During mealtimes it was customary for the speakers to sit at different tables with different ministers so they would have an opportunity to fellowship with the speakers. Some of the conversations were lively and amusing and some left one wondering what planet people lived on! It has always been my view that if a man is secure in his ministry he doesn't need to fight for silly doctrines but is able to discuss things in an open way.

One day, my wife and I walked into lunch and ended up sitting opposite a husband and wife who looked totally depressed. One could see from their faces that joy had eluded them and a cloud hung over them.

I thought, as I sat down, "Oh dear." These poor people looked so miserable.

After some introductions and casual talk we got down to talking about the conference and the way the meetings were going.

The man looked over at me and said, "Tell me, you have miracles in your ministry. What did you do to get the gift? Did you fast and pray? What's your secret?"

I replied, "I never did anything. Gifts are given by God. The Holy Spirit chooses whom He will. I just found miracles happened. I never sought a gift. The callings of God are His callings. How shall a preacher go unless he's sent. It's God who is Lord of His church and gives gifted men to minister."

"Well," he said, "I don't believe that. My wife and I went to a Word of Faith College and we want a healing ministry. We decided to seek earnestly and both of us fasted forty days and forty nights to get a gift of healing."

"OK," I said, "and what was the result of your forty days fasting? I must commend you for your efforts but what did it produce?"

His face turned more miserable, if that were possible, and he said, "Nothing. We came up empty. Nothing happened."

Intrigued by this, I asked, "So what did you do next?"

"Someone told us that obviously we needed to seek God more, so my wife and I decided that we should fast and pray again for forty days and nights and then God would hear us."

I was impressed. Here was a dear couple who had twice set themselves to fast forty days and nights. Surely something must have happened. I asked him, "Well, what was the result of your second effort?"

He looked at me quite forlorn and replied, "It didn't work. We came up dry again. We dug our well but there was no water. We thought God would have to give us the gift but nothing worked. For two years now we've tried everything and nothing works. What's your secret?"

As I looked across at them I felt so sorry for them and wondered how I could help without hurting them.

"Well, my friend," I said, "I think you need to understand one thing, clearly God hasn't called you to the ministry because whom He calls He always equips. You can starve yourself to death before you can get God to do what He doesn't want to do. Ministry is to do with the call of God, not with my ambitions or desires. My suggestion is you find a job and join a good church where God's Spirit is moving. God loves you. He doesn't want to frustrate you, nor destroy you. If we try to manipulate God to get our own way, we fail. We need to find out what He wants and become co-workers together with him."

"Let me tell you something else," he said. "We went to a conference three years ago and heard about 'sowing seed.' The preachers gave many examples of how you could sow to reap a harvest. We gave our Pontiac car to a minister. He didn't have a car so we 'sowed our seed' in faith, believing that God would provide a new Cadillac."

Curiosity got the better of me. "So, what happened?" I asked.

Crestfallen, he looked across at me and said, "It didn't work. We had to go on the bus for the next two and a half years."

I asked him how old the Pontiac was.

"Eight years old." But he had expected a brand new Cadillac in its place!

I told him the seed we sow is the word of God and the harvest is assured, but to try and manipulate God in such a way as he had tried wasn't right.

I asked him the most important question that anyone could be asked, "Do you really know what God wants for you and your wife? You've spent years trying to get what you want. Isn't it about time you sought His will and found out what He really wants for you? Life's so wonderful when we flow in the will of God and so miserable when we try to manipulate things to get our will."

He looked at me and said, "I'm claiming the scriptures and standing on the promises of God."

I pointed out, "There's a lot of difference between a living word of God and the dead letter. The letter killeth but the Spirit giveth life. A leper told to dip seven times in Jordan finally obeyed and came up cleansed, but it isn't the cure for all leprosy. It was spoken to one man who obeyed. You can't take scriptures and apply them to yourself if God doesn't apply them and speak them by His Spirit. Jesus came to give us life and life more abundant, but that abundant life is in the will of the Father, not our will. He has a perfect plan for every life but it's only as we pray and bring our hearts into union with His will that we truly taste that abundant life."

I told him, "Your experiences have taught you how empty lofty ambition and self-seeking can be. God hasn't cast you off but you need to humble yourself under the mighty hand of God so you can hear His voice and find out His purpose."

They left the conference the next day, mad because they had failed to find the solution that they wanted. It seemed as if they didn't want to hear the truth. I felt sorry for them.

I have met so many people who have been as faithful as they know how to be, as diligent as they know how to be, as dedicated as they know how to be. Unfortunately, though they find it hard to admit, they are following their own ambitions, their own purposes, their own drives, instead of falling in love with Jesus, following Him and fulfilling His will.

Jesus Christ has come to lift us up. He has not come to judge and condemn us. He's come to bring hope and life more abundant. Many ask what they can do to gain this life. The answer is, nothing. You must repent: that means to turn from the way you're living and receive the gift of the Holy Spirit. Repentance is a free gift. *"For by grace are ye saved through faith; and that not of yourselves: it is the gift of God" (Eph. 2:8).*

You don't have to do anything for it, since Christ paid the

price 2,000 years ago on Calvary's Tree.   A gift is not
something you can earn, claim or take.   It's something God
sovereignly gives.   He loves us.   He has a purpose for each
one of us, but we must be humble enough and willing enough
to do what He wants, instead of demanding what we want.
Grace is totally undeserved favour.   I can't help but see my
Jesus as full of grace and truth.   He's a good God.   He doesn't
want me to afflict my soul or my body to earn what is so free.

Let me give you an example.   I have a grandson called
Gideon.   When he was six years old, he was staying in my
home with his parents and sister for a while.

One breakfast in November he came to the table and looked
at me and said, "Grandpa, I've got a catalogue here with what
I want for Christmas.   Is it too expensive or can you afford to
buy it for me?"

He had put a little sticky label on the page and told me it
would be easier for me to find what he wanted.   It was mid-
November but my little grandson had already planned out his
Christmas.

"Can you afford it?" he asked.

When I looked at the catalogue I saw that what he wanted
was a typical toy for a boy and would have done him no harm
at all.   I knew it would give him pleasure and also encourage
his imagination so I was happy to tell him, "Yeah, I can afford
that."

He smiled and said, "Well, if you can afford that, how about
everything on the page?"

I laughed.

He said, "Grandpa, you can keep the catalogue so you
remember what I want."

When Christmas came he got what he wanted, plus a few more things off the page. He didn't earn it. He didn't do anything for it. He just knew Grandpa loved him and couldn't resist his smile.

Jesus said, *"Except ye be converted, and become as little children, ye shall not enter into the kingdom of heaven" (Matt. 18:3)*. My grandson knew he didn't need to earn favour. He didn't need to manipulate, and he trusted his grandfather because he understood that a gift is a gift, and when it is a gift, it doesn't cost anything. He knew Grandpa would pay the price.

How hard it is to get Christians to understand that Jesus paid the price for everything. If only we could become like little children and put our trust in Him who has done it all!

Preaching the simple Gospel.

6

It's a Gift!

My heart's desire is to bring people to a realisation of what God has already done for them, so that they can become partakers of the inheritance which was laid up before the foundation of the world. The Bible teaches in Ephesians 1 verse 3 that we have been blessed with *all* spiritual blessings in heavenly places. It's already done, Christ accomplished it all on Calvary's Tree 2,000 years ago. The Book of Romans exhorts us to reckon ourselves dead unto sin but alive unto God. We died with Christ; we rose with Him.

On the day of Pentecost, Peter made it plain: it's the gift of the Holy Spirit that's given to bring us into life. God so loved the world that He gifted His only begotten Son. God came to do something for us because we cannot help ourselves.

The Bible records how Jesus died for us while we were yet enemies of God, alienated from the life of God. The natural mind is enmity against God. Everything within us from our natural birth militates against the very God of creation. We're born in depravity with a depraved nature and yet the grace of God reaches to should care for us or be mindful of us, except for His bountiful love and grace.

Like many people, I went to see the film, *The Passion*, and although I didn't agree with some of it, I could not but wonder at the amazing love of God to allow His Son to suffer so much for us, to endure the ignominy of crucifixion, to allow Him to be beaten nigh unto death. The film vividly portrayed the violence of crucifixion. How could such a loving God care so much for us when we were His enemies?

I came out of the cinema full of wonder at the grace of God, that undeserved favour, which dug me out of a horrible pit. Jesus took our sin and pain on Calvary and by the predetermined counsel of God suffered for us. How could mankind ignore such a wonderful salvation offered, the price having already been paid?

Religion demands that we must fulfill certain conditions in order to receive blessing from God. God is always presented as austere and far away. He is always portrayed as an angry God and only our right actions will placate Him. I find many Christians have this attitude towards God and feel that if they let Him down, some great disaster is waiting to happen.

A contemporary author writes that God can't do what He wants to do in the world if we don't pray enough. He claims God's power is limited through lack of prayer. What absolute absurdity! My God is almighty and everything in creation is upheld by the word of His power. He has all power and all authority; in heaven, in earth and under the earth.

It's not what we can do for God; it's what He wants to do for us. He is the Alpha and Omega of our faith. He is the one who has come to give us abundant life. He is the Redeemer, the Saviour. He is the eternal mighty God and every good thing comes from Him.

When I visit African nations I'm often horrified at the

burdens that are put on the shoulders of oppressed people. If they fast enough, pray enough and give enough money then God will meet them.

Recently, at a crusade in Cameroon, I told the people that they didn't need to pray and fast for seven days to get healed, it was a free gift of God. They didn't need to bring a brown envelope with money to the man of God; healing was a free gift. I told them to eat a good meal and come to the meeting rejoicing because God loved them and miracles would happen because of what Christ had already done.

The people cheered and came to the meetings. It was wonderful to watch blind eyes open, deaf ears unstop, cripples walk and growths vanish. All done by the grace of God. We can't earn anything because the price has been paid by Jesus. Miracles happen when redemption is preached.

Many preachers lay tremendous burdens on people they wouldn't touch with their little finger. Thank God that Jesus came to remove the burden! Religion increases the burdens and makes us struggle to escape our bondages. Christianity proclaims the good news that we can be free because of what He's done.

Let me tell you an incident that happened a few years ago in Accra, Ghana. I was holding a mission in the Methodist Cathedral. Miracles happened night after night and the crowd swelled so that we had to move to an adjoining building. One side of the building opened onto a field where we put up a big projector and screens so that the crowds outside could see what was going on and hear the gospel. The campaign was due to finish on the Friday night but so many people were coming we decided to hold a Saturday night meeting as well.

On that Saturday the crowds were immense, the building was filled and the crowds outside were increasing by the minute. In the first part of the meeting we had singing and rejoicing. God had been so good, many people had been healed and delivered.

A non-Christian woman was in a local bar nearby when she heard singing like she'd never heard before. She wondered what the noise was and even though she was very drunk, she decided to find out what was going on. She staggered out of the bar and across the field towards the crowd and the light. By the time she arrived at the back of the crowd, I was preaching about the God of the impossible.

As I spoke about Jesus healing the sick, she reasoned within herself, "If this Jesus can do the impossible maybe He can heal my withered arm."

Her left arm had been withered from birth. She began to push through the crowd to get to the front. As I prayed for the sick and invited those who were healed to come to the front, this woman finally made her way through the crowd to the edge of the platform. To her absolute shock, she found that her left arm had grown out to be completely normal like her right arm.

She was so excited at what God had done she attempted to climb on to the platform to tell everyone. I shall never forget the chaos that ensued.

This dear woman, drunk as she was, bellowed to the congregation, "You all know me. My left arm was withered. I was born that way and look what God has done for me."

She began waving the arm that was healed but, being so drunk, she overbalanced and I watched as she collapsed, taking two bishops down with her. We got her up on her feet and helped the bishops up, but she insisted on waving her arm and went straight over the drum kit, sending everything flying. Her excitement was infectious but her drunkenness was uncontrollable. We retrieved her from the midst of the drums and sat her on a chair with a woman on each side to calm her. Jesus Christ had healed her.

I realised that had she arrived for prayer at the front in such a state of drunkenness, I would have suggested that she come back when she was sober. Our God knew better than that and His grace reached through to her need, and healed her in spite of her drunken state. What love and mercy our God shows in reaching to the depths of depravity with love and tenderness! Jesus hasn't come to condemn the world but to save and to lift up.

The next morning that same woman turned up at the Cathedral totally sober. She had brought her whole family with her and declared that she would never drink again and had come to give her heart and life to Christ, the one who had healed her so beautifully. What a change!

The Bible says, it's the goodness of God that leads to repentance, not judgmental wrath and religious strictures imposed on people. How strange that our God would meet a drunken woman with such grace. His nature is always to forgive and lift up, never to condemn.

It has been my experience around the world that the gospel of Jesus Christ preached in the power of the Spirit can meet every need. I've seen it happen time and again in many campaigns all over the world. It's a gift of God's own Son. Very often the people in most desperate need with no religious background accept Christ with grateful hearts whilst the religious people sit by as critics and detractors; hasn't it always been that way?

"For by grace are ye saved through faith; and that not of yourselves: it is the gift of God" (Eph. 2:8).

In Italy, a young boy is healed from a terrible stutter.

7

Kids Too!

In the early days of our church I determined that I was not going to sink down into the religious norms of the day where children were taught that church was for grownups and children's meetings were put on to entertain them whilst the service and preaching went on. To me, it meant that subconsciously children were taught that church was only for adults and 'fuddy-duddies' and they were to be excluded. What a terrible message it all implied.

My wife and I decided that we would have the children in the church so they could watch the miracles, see God work and listen to the preaching. Spurgeon, that great man of God, said that if a five year old could not understand a preacher then he was preaching over people's heads. How true that is!

Isn't it amazing that God's plan for the family was that they should talk about the things of God at all times, wherever they were. Christ was to be central and the things of God discussed. Amazingly, at 12 years old, Jesus was in the temple reasoning with the scribes and Pharisees and High Priests. They were astonished at His understanding. His parents found that He was quite at home debating with theologians, even at the age of 12. One must ask how many churches would allow 12 year olds to discuss the deep things of God. How many families talk about the beauties of Christ in their homes?

Whilst on a mission trip to Italy, we had a healing crusade in a church near Naples. The crowds were so big that the overflow hall was filled and people were left in the car park because so many came when they heard about the miracles.

On the last night, we witnessed a beautiful miracle. A young boy was there, only 11 years old. He had been unable to speak because of a terrible stutter. During the service he came up onto the stage with his face shining and a bright smile, thrilled that this Jesus he had heard about had totally delivered him and now he was free he could speak publicly. His stutter had completely gone! His mother said he had never been able to talk to anyone without the terrible stammering, but because he had been allowed into the church and listened to the gospel, Jesus Christ had met him and totally healed him. It was a joy to see his response.

I thought how wonderful it was that all the young children were in the church to hear the gospel. It's quite amazing how open they are when they're not patronised. Jesus Christ said, *"Suffer little children to come unto me, and forbid them not" (Lk. 18:16)*.

According to Christian Research UK, during the 1990s, over 1,000 young people a week under the age of 15 stopped going to church; that is, over 50,000 children a year severed their connection with churches. I believe one of the main reasons for this is the failure of families to really acknowledge the spiritual needs of their children and the lack of care to bring them up in the fear and admonition of God.

Very often the television becomes the babysitter and normal conversation and communication breaks down in the home. Parents no longer communicate with each other and fail to really communicate with their children. It's little wonder that by their teenage years children are saying their parents don't understand them. They've never communicated as they grew up. In a true church with a Christian family it should never be this way.

How often I think of people like Count Zinzendorf, a leading Moravian, whose son at the age of five was writing hymns which were doctrinally sound and musically beautiful. In England most five year olds would only know nursery rhymes or computer games. We need to get back to the command of God to train up our children in the way they should go. We need to realise our responsibility to the church of tomorrow: to train the children of today in the ways of God.

Christianity is a joyous life, not an austere and restrictive one. Christ came to give us life and life more abundant, not to impinge upon our liberties. He came to liberate us from the harmful snares of the enemy so that we could enjoy abundance with total freedom from the ravages of sin. His intention is always that we should share continuous fellowship with Him and know Him as He really is.

What a travesty that this wonderful Saviour, one tender enough for children to feel comfortable in His presence and to seek blessing from, should be portrayed as distant and austere by some 'over religious' churches.

Christ came to earth to reveal the heart of God and change things around so that the precepts of men and the self-righteousness that accompanies religion would be banished forever; that judgmental condemnation would be superceded by loving grace; that condemnation would be swallowed up with the revelation of the forgiveness of God and the restoration of His image in the heart. What a beautiful gospel we have when we shake ourselves free from the dark cloak of religion!

When our children were growing up they used to find bath times great fun. They would 'baptise' each other in the bath and would strongly rebuke each other if they didn't come up out of the water 'speaking in tongues.' At prayer times they expected miracles to happen and expected answers to prayer. For them, Christianity was great fun. When they played with their friends they'd often set up a pulpit and preach to the other children. It was part of their life and a great part of their understanding.

Carolyn Scott, in her biography about the Maréchale, recounts similar behaviour in the home of William Booth, founder of the Salvation Army. "Nursery games consisted of preaching, heckling, and dragging to the penitent bench: 'Give up the drink, brother!' Ballington preached to pillows, bashing them into submission, while his sisters watched spellbound with their dolls in their arms, 'Take the babies out of the theatre', being countered indignantly with 'Papa wouldn't have stopped. Papa would have gone on preaching!'" To them, "singing and praying and talk of salvation were part of daily life as natural as eating and sleeping." (The Heavenly Witch, The Story of the Maréchale by Carolyn Scott, 1981, Hamish Hamilton Ltd).

When it came to reading, our children read popular authors such as Enid Blyton, but they grew to love the stories of missionaries, such as Hudson Taylor and Mary Slessor, which my wife read to them every night. By the age of 8 or 9 they would go into my library to borrow books of missionary tales.

To them it was more exciting than anything. We would often sit down at meal times and questions would fly. At night time they would always discuss Bible stories.   To them, the kingdom of God was a beautiful place and the secrets of God's work were a treasure to them.

Crippled no more, the man from the hotel lobby...

8

It's Not Magic!

V ery often I find people equate the miracle ministry with a type of magic and they separate the truth of the gospel from the miracles of healing and transformation. They seem to feel that a minister who has a particular gift can function in any circumstance just praying for people without any reference to the truths of the gospel or the demand for a changed life.

We need to understand that the good news of the gospel is the power of God unto salvation and that healing flows in the truth of the Gospel. Let me explain with a little story.

I was in Cameroon to hold a crusade in the city centre of Yaounde. The first night thousands came, with many miracles of healing. Over 500 people responded by giving their lives to Christ. The miracles happened in the midst of it all; blind eyes opened, deaf mutes healed, cancers vanished. It was a wonderful night. We returned to our hotel rejoicing in what God had done.

The next day, I came down to the hotel lobby to go for some lunch and saw a crippled man in the hall. He could barely walk. My wife and I passed into the dining room and sat down at a table with some ministers. The crippled man approached slowly, dragging one leg and clearly in pain.

He asked, "Are you the Bishop who's praying for people and seeing the miracles?"

I said, "I am."

He then said, "Pray for me, I'm crippled. I need God to heal me."

I told him, "You need to come to the meeting tonight and hear the gospel and God will heal you."

"No," he said, "I just want to be healed now. You can pray for me here in the hotel. I don't need to go to any gospel meeting."

I said, "I'm sorry, I'm going to have lunch and there's no way I'm going to pray for you unless you come to the gospel meeting. God will heal you there."

He got a little angry and said, "Listen, I paid to fly to Germany to see a well-known evangelist. It cost me a lot of money and he prayed for me personally for half an hour. Nothing happened. He said I'd be healed but I wasn't. He deceived me."

I told him, "If you'll come to the meeting tonight, I promise you, after the gospel's preached, God will heal you. It won't take half an hour to pray. God will heal you within 30 seconds."

He turned away from me, saying, "I don't believe that. I can't get to the meeting," and then he left the dining room.

That night, when I arrived at the open air meeting, the crowds were flocking and, to my delight, I saw the gentleman on the front row. As I mounted the platform, he waved to me. He'd come for his miracle. As I preached, I realised the Spirit of God had moved upon him and when I made the call for people to give their hearts to Christ he came forward, slowly and haltingly. He had to push through the crowd to get near the platform.

I looked down at him and said, "I promised you God would heal you. Begin to move your crippled leg. His power is here."

He bent his knee and began to move his leg. He said, "The pain's gone!"

I told him, "Run up the platform." He ran up the stairs and across the platform, totally healed.

I said to him, "I told you it would only take 30 seconds. God is in Cameroon. You didn't need to go to Germany and spend all that money. Jesus is here." It was wonderful to see him saved and healed by the grace of God.

The next day when I came down for lunch I was astonished to see this man standing in the lobby, waiting for me. He ran up, laughing, and said, "Look, I'm healed. I'm healed, so I've brought my son. He needs a miracle, pray for him."

I said to him, "What's wrong?"

"He can't bend over. He injured his back in a fall. He's in constant pain."

I laughed and said to him, "You remember you had to come to the meeting to hear the gospel? Well, so has your son."

He replied, "I heard the gospel last night. My son doesn't need it." I pointed out to him there was no way I was going to pray for him except on the crusade ground.

That night, when I arrived at the crusade ground, I laughed to see my dear friend with his son, sitting on the front row, waiting for their miracle. When the gospel was preached, his son came forward, and as I prayed a general prayer, he was completely healed. How wonderful it was to see a father and son, running, jumping, hugging, and shouting for joy.

The next day, I came down to the lobby for lunch, and there he was again! This time, with his other son, who'd got large boils under his arm and an abscess. He couldn't put his arm down by his side. We went through the same routine and lo and behold, that night, his other son was instantly healed. The boils and abscess just vanished. He was so happy.

You'd have thought that would be the end of the matter, but not so. The next day, I found him in the lobby again! This time, with his two daughters whom he said really needed to get saved. Surely, this time I'd lay hands on them, since he'd been to the meeting three times and they only wanted to get saved, having seen the miracles that God had done for the family. I pointed out to him that the gospel is the power of God unto salvation and if they wanted to get saved they'd better be at the meeting that night.

Sure enough, they were, and they got gloriously filled with the Holy Spirit. What a happy father he was, with two sons healed and his daughters saved. The father, who was once a cripple, leapt and jumped for joy. It was such a beautiful sight. They hugged and laughed and cried together, rejoicing in what God had done for them.

Many miracles happened in Cameroon and God's power was displayed. Over 300 pastors attended the meetings every morning and heard the word of God. Their unanimous comment was, "We never knew the gospel was so simple and that miracles are so easy. We never appreciated what redemption meant." They begged me to come back again.

All over the world, I find many Christians who believe in the miracle power of God but don't see the miracles happening in their churches. I believe it's because they don't understand that faith comes by hearing the word of God and that miracle power flows when the word of God is preached in the power of the Spirit.

I tell people, "if you go to a church where you don't see miracles: blind eyes opening, deaf ears unstopping, cripples running, then you haven't found a church yet."

'No miracles, … No Jesus.'

Wherever Jesus is, miracles happen. He hasn't changed in 2,000 years. He sent His disciples to preach, teach and heal and He's given us the same commission: to bring His life, love and liberty to a sin-sick world. Something good is going to happen because God loves you. He really cares. He sent His Son to buy your redemption with His own precious blood.

He meets every need because He's a good God. A God of love and a God of grace and there's nothing you need to do – It's so easy!

Christ did it all...

9

Good News!

n 1986 a couple turned up at our church at the invitation of friends who were church members. They had been through a very traumatic experience. A week before they visited us, their youngest child, a baby, had died of cot death. When the child died, they rang their pastor who told them to call the elders to pray to raise the baby from the dead. They obeyed, and for some hours the elders prayed over the corpse.

Nothing happened!

When nothing happened, they believed, in line with what they had been taught, that their lack of faith meant they had lost their child. It was their fault! When I spoke to them they were still in a state of shock but, more than that, they were in deep pain because of what they'd been told.

False teaching brings so much suffering to people's minds and hearts. The Scripture says that 'time and chance' happen to every man. Cot deaths are tragic happenings but let me explain why what they had been taught was so wrong.

Firstly, the Bible says that Jesus has the keys to death and hell, not the devil. It is appointed unto man once to die and that appointment no one will miss. That appointment is in God the Father's hands, not the devil's. Our God is a good God but we do not know His eternal purposes. As Christians we submit to the will of God knowing that *"all things work together for good to them that love God" (Rom. 8:28).*

Tragic as this incident was for the family, God restored them wonderfully over the next year. He healed their hurts and has continued to intervene in their lives with miraculous healings for the family.

Secondly, we have a gospel of good news! In the face of adversity we often find the hand of God is working to our benefit. The tragic circumstance delivered them from false teaching and brought them to a true faith in Christ. One can never explain why things happen. When Jesus was questioned why a man was blind, whether it was his sin or his parents, He rebuked the disciples for thinking that way and said it was for the glory of God.

Today, many Christians are superstitious and are always looking for a reason for sickness or disease. I always tell people, "There is only one reason why you're sick and that is because you're not well. If you were well you wouldn't be sick."

Often, ministers tell people they're cursed by what their grandfathers or fathers have done. The scripture denies this. Isaiah says that although the fathers eat sour grapes the children's teeth will not be set on edge. Generational curses come down only to those who hate God.

A short time ago, a dear elderly couple who needed healing visited our church. God met them gloriously and healed them. Whilst chatting to them afterwards, they told me a tragic story. Three of their grandchildren had been diagnosed as dyslexic. They sought prayer from their local ministry and were told that because the grandfather had been a Freemason 18 years ago, this had brought the calamity of dyslexia on the children. The poor man felt tremendous guilt because of what he was *supposed to* have inflicted on his grandchildren.

What the pastor said was not true. Firstly, in Galatians it makes it clear that witchcraft (Freemasonry) is only a work of the flesh. Secondly, generational curses do not apply to Christians at all. When we're born again we're totally delivered from all curses because Jesus became a curse for us when He hung on the cross.

In my book, *Strategic Level Spiritual Warfare: A Modern Mythology?*, I have addressed these issues. How terrible for a dear grandfather to be told that he'd cursed his grandchildren with no hope for an answer.

When we become Christians we don't have a past, we have a glorious future. When we're born again of God's Spirit, God divides our sin as far as the east is from the west and remembers it no more. If God remembers it no more, how could He possibly curse the person or their descendants? It would make God a liar for us to believe such things. My Bible says that the blood of Jesus Christ, God's Son, cleanses us from all unrighteousness.

The gospel of Jesus Christ is one of hope and deliverance! It's good news! Our God sent His Son not to condemn the world for past actions but that all would be saved through His sacrifice on Calvary's tree. He's a gracious God. He came to dig us out of the miry clay not to push our faces in it. He heals the sick, delivers the captive, forgives sin, and makes us partakers of His divine nature. We have proof that He can lift people up. It is hope for the hopeless. He's the answer to all we need in life.

It is time for Christians to abandon superstition and fear and walk in the face of what Christ has done for them.

I was so thrilled to see that grandfather totally set free from the guilt and fear that had been foisted on him by false teaching. I was so thrilled to see the family who'd lost a baby through cot death restored to the realisation of the love and mercy of God and set free from the guilt and shame of supposed failure, namely their lack of faith. Thousands of Christians today are hurt by false teaching.

Let me exhort you to realise that God is on your side. He's a good God. He loves you. Jesus Christ has done everything necessary to bring about total restoration in your life.

Let us shake off what I call 'Christian witchcraft' and live in the fullness of what Jesus has done for us. Let us return to the simplicity of the gospel which is in Jesus Christ. It truly is an abundant life!

As easy as A, B, C...

10

It's So Easy!

Time and time again people say to me, "Why is Christianity so complicated? I found it very easy to become a Christian, but once I joined a church everything became very complicated. There are so many doctrines that are hard to understand and every church seems to have a different interpretation of the Bible; it makes living the Christian life so difficult."

One of the most common statements I hear when people come to our church is "You make it so simple, so practical – I can really understand it."

You may wonder what the contrast is, but I think it would be helpful if I explained in simple terms the things that make the difference. When I was converted I was born again and received a totally new life, partaking of the divine nature, when the Lord sovereignly spoke into my being.

It was in that moment I realised that it was God who did everything and I had done nothing:

He changed me;

He healed me;

He cleansed me;

He forgave me;

He transformed my inward nature;

He imparted His life into my being.

He did it all because He is the Saviour. I did absolutely nothing but I found He had become my sufficiency. It was so simple. He is the Alpha and Omega, the beginning and the end. He is the author and finisher of our faith – what a wonderful Saviour He is!

After I got saved, people who called themselves Christians tried to overload me with rules and regulations of their own imagination. They wanted to impose upon me their cultural take on what a Christian should be. Truly, I felt like the man who had fallen amongst thieves. They attempted to rob me of my liberty and told me I had to earn the things which previously I had been given so freely.

Two thousand years ago Jesus went to Calvary; He died on the cross to deal with sin. He took your sin and my sin into his own body on the tree. The Bible says *"For he hath made him to be sin for us, who knew no sin; that we might be made the righteousness of God in him." (2 Cor. 5:21).*

Nothing anyone does can add to the atonement; Jesus did it once and for all. We are not forgiven on the basis of what we do but on what He did for us. No one can negate what He did for us and He gives us the benefits of what He did for us two thousand years ago.

It is so simple and so wonderful!

Two thousand years ago He rose from the dead on the third day. He came out of the tomb, having been raised by the glory of the Father, and that same power that raised Him from the dead, works in us today, causing us to partake of His very nature. We are born again not of the will of man nor of the flesh, we are born again of God, by God, through God – the author and finisher of our faith. It is so easy and so simple!

Two thousand years ago He ascended into Heaven and presented His precious blood to atone for all our sins. It is through His precious blood that we are cleansed and forgiven. On the day of Pentecost, He poured out His Holy Spirit on all flesh and the Church was born.

He has never withdrawn His Spirit nor abandoned His true church. We have a rich inheritance that He has given us and we can enjoy all the benefits of His redemption because He has done a perfect work. We have inherited what He purchased for us. It is so simple!

Two thousand years ago, when He hung on a tree, the Bible says He became a curse for us because cursed is everyone who hangs on a tree. He not only became sin, He became a curse and so in His death and resurrection He broke the power of sin and every curse for us. It is part of the redemption story.

Today I hear of so many people who are misled by false teaching and even though they are Christians they are told that they are under generational curses that need to be broken. That is a lie of the devil – when we are born again we are born free! All we need to do is believe what Jesus has already done for us and live in the fullness of it. It is so easy!

Two thousand years ago He birthed the Church at Pentecost with a clear promise that the gates of hell would not prevail against it. The gospel, the good news of what He has done for us, is the power of salvation to everyone who will believe it. When we accept what Christ has done for us, the truth of the gospel has a transforming power in us. I have travelled the world over and seen the miracle working power of a miracle working God. He meets our needs because He loves and cares for us – Jesus Christ is God's gift to the world.

It *is* so easy!! Remember salvation is a gift and Jesus paid the price so you may receive the gift freely. What great news! God bless you. Just keep it simple and trust what He has done for you!

It's so easy!

Michael Reid Ministries

MIRACLES·HEALING·FAITH

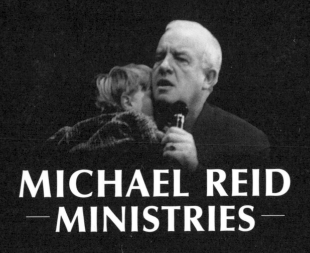

MICHAEL REID
—MINISTRIES—

Building on the foundation of our biblically based family ethos, and
our focus on miracles, healing and faith, the church expands under
God-anointed leadership. With the Word of God as our touchstone, we
are a voice to the nations through evangelism, education and excellence

PENIEL CHURCH

Founded by Michael and Ruth Reid as a small bible study group in their front room in 1976, Peniel Church, with connections worldwide, has grown to hundreds of members.

Peniel was the place where Jacob met face to face with God. Peniel Church has seen many experience that same face to face meeting.

The Peniel church congregation is made up of a huge variety of cultures, age groups and nationalities all united by their belief in Jesus Christ their Saviour. God has intervened in people's lives to bring them together as one huge family with Him as their Father and Bishop Reid as their pastor.

PENIEL COLLEGE OF HIGHER EDUCATION

Affiliated with Oral Roberts University and in Partnership with the University of Wales, Bangor, the college's motto is:

"Study to shew thyself approved unto God, a workman who needeth not to be ashamed, rightly dividing the word of truth." (II Timothy 2 v 15)

This Scripture birthed in Michael Reid's heart the vision for the College.

In 1997, Michael Reid was appointed an Associate Regent of Oral Roberts University and in the same year, the College gained a unique affiliation to Oral Roberts University in Tulsa, Oklahoma, USA.

Peniel College of Higher Education is now the only campus in the UK authorised by Oral Roberts University and the North Central Accrediting Association, to be able to offer degree courses.

Michael Reid is also a trustee on the board of the International Charismatic Bible Ministries (ICBM) chaired by Richard Roberts.

In 2005, Peniel College obtained partnership with the University of Wales, Bangor, enabling students to graduate with UK accredited Bachelors or Masters degrees.

THE GLOBAL GOSPEL FELLOWSHIP

Global Gospel Fellowship was birthed after Bishop Reid and TL Osborn talked about their own experiences as world travelled preachers. As they fellowshipped together in Puerto Rico they began to discuss the need for an organisation which would encourage fellowship amongst Christian leadership; fellowship that would not only enrich people spiritually but would be a practical help to church leaders across the globe.

Global Gospel Fellowship was founded in 2000 as an interdenominational forum providing fellowship and teaching for church leaders who believe that the God of miracles still intervenes today. Each year, Michael Reid Ministries hosts the annual GGF conference attended by pastors from across the globe. Speakers such as TL Osborn, Bill Wilson, Charles Green, Paul Dhinakaran and Rev V Dilkumar give direction and share at these events.

PENIEL TV

"Jesus always took his message to the people and in this modern age, television provides us with a fantastic opportunity to do the same by taking His Word right into people's homes." - Bishop Reid

Peniel's unique TV show "What God Can Do For You" was first aired in 2002. It has gone from strength to strength and is now broadcast into 5 continents from Australia, to Africa, to Europe, to Asia and to North America. The shows are packed with miracle testimonies, practical teaching, lively discussion and ministry by the Peniel Choir and are also streamed worldwide on the internet, via the Michael Reid Ministries Website (www.MichaelReidMinistries.org).

PENIEL CHOIR

The Peniel Choir started in 1989 with 23 people. Today, it has more than 100 choristers, all of whom are committed Church members.

Members range from 18 year-old students to grandparents, from housewives to company directors. They are people who want to promote Jesus in song, to support the ministry of Michael Reid and to challenge their hearers with the Gospel message.

The choir ministers weekly at the Sunday 10am service, and travels with Bishop Michael Reid in the UK and abroad. They have recorded a number of albums; see our website for details.

PENIEL ACADEMY SCHOOL

One of Bishop Reid's desires is to ensure that the youth of today become the church of tomorrow. Peniel Academy was started as an offshoot of the church and the aim has always been for the children to become functioning members of God's church globally. The school is open to children of church members and caters for children of varying abilities from nursery to school-leaving age.

Starting with a roll of just seventeen pupils, the school has now grown to over one hundred and fifty, and its expansion has seen it move to the magnificent 74-acre site at Brizes Park on the outskirts of Brentwood.

The school was founded from the very start on two principles. Firstly, the school should be based firmly on a Bible ethos. Secondly, there should be one standard in the home, the church and the school. Each is inter-dependent on each other and this unique cooperation is a tremendous recipe for success.

The emphasis in the school is on excellence. Behind such a core belief lies total dedication - staff and parents who are astonishingly committed. Their focus is to achieve the best for the children in a holistic way - body, mind and spirit. There is the constant expectation that all children can achieve their full potential in sport, in academics and in their enjoyment of life.

Most fundamentally, the cornerstone of the school is its Christian belief which delivers a clear moral standard and code of behaviour. Pupils are inspired by staff who are a living testimony to honesty, industry and personal integrity.

WEBSITE

The website started as a couple of pages in June 1996. It has grown to an accumulation of articles, audio sermons, video downloads and much more.

The internet has provided another forum to promote the gospel and spread the good news of Jesus Christ. As the number of people looking at the website increases, we are getting many more e-mails of support, questions and prayer requests. Once again it is a fantastic opportunity to take the gospel into people's homes.

www.MichaelReidMinistries.org

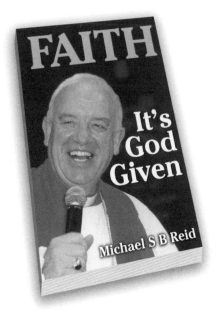 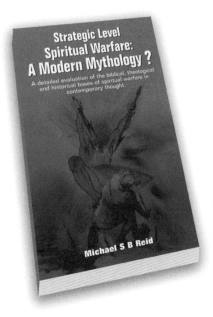

Faith: It's God Given

This book, packed with dynamic illustrations and truths of scripture, is written for those who are sick of the false "faith" emphasis that condemns and discourages, and will realign your thinking to the true Biblical faith in Christ.

The inspired simplicity of Bishop Reid's message brings a new hope and understanding as he urges his readers to abandon their understanding and accept that GOD ALONE CAN DO IT.

Order: UK: +44(0)1277 372996 USA: 918-491-2078

Strategic Level Spiritual Warfare: A Modern Mythology?

"Don't touch this, it's Dangerous!"

Don't read this book if you are not prepared to examine the Biblical base for your practices.

Strategic Level Spiritual Warfare (SLSW) has evolved from a radical change in the perception of spiritual warfare which has developed over the last thirty years. It is widely practised by many in the Christian community around the world. Does it have any foundation in the Word of God, the Bible?

If you are searching for the whole truth about what Jesus did for you on Calvary and you want to know how to practise true spiritual warfare then this book is for you!

The concepts and teaching of SLSW have drawn people away from the eternal truths of scripture. This book refocuses people's understanding on what the Bible teaches about spiritual warfare, enabling believers to live and walk in Christ's total victory over the devil and all demonic powers, which He won at Calvary.

Michael Reid examines in depth the SLSW movement which bases its teaching on the evaluation of experience and anecdotal evidence.

www.MichaelReidMinistries.org

INVITATION

You are warmly invited to attend Church services at
Michael Reid Ministries, in the UK, every Sunday at 10am.

UK: +44 (0) 1277 372996

USA: 918-491-2078

e-mail: sunday10am@peniel.org

UK:

Michael Reid Ministries

49 Coxtie Green Road

Brentwood

Essex CM14 5PS

England

USA:

Michael Reid Ministries

PO BOX 702220

TULSA OKLAHOMA 74170

ABOUT THE AUTHOR

Founder of Michael Reid Ministries, Bishop Michael Reid is a tireless ambassador for the Kingdom of God. His determination to obey God whatever the cost, his uncompromising preaching of the Word, and his strong convictions have moulded the church and its ministries. It is through his clear presentation of the gospel that many worldwide have come to know Jesus Christ as their Saviour and experience His healing power in their lives.

Today thousands throughout the world can testify of God's healing power which has touched their lives through this man who declares, "I cannot heal you, I cannot change your circumstances but I know One who can – His name is Jesus, and He lives in me!"

The bedrock of Michael Reid Ministries is Peniel Church, founded in 1976. Michael is also principal of Peniel Academy, President of Peniel College (affiliated with Oral Roberts University (ORU) and in partnership with the University of Wales) and founder of the Global Gospel Fellowship. He is also a Regent on the board of ORU and a Trustee of the International Charismatic Bible Ministries.

He has recently formed, with other church leaders and lay Christians, the Christian Congress for Traditional Values which seeks to uphold Christian values within the UK. Michael has authored several other books including the highly acclaimed *Strategic Level Spiritual Warfare: A Modern Mythology?* He and his wife, Ruth, host their own television programme "What God Can Do For You" which reaches people throughout the world with the gospel.

Michael and Ruth live in Essex and have three grown-up children. Michael has an earned Doctor of Ministry and an honorary Doctor of Divinity from Oral Roberts University.